AF379588

GETTING THINGS DONE AND STAYING ORGANISED

Increase productivity and banish procrastination

Written by Isabelle Aussant

Translated by Carly Probert

50MINUTES.com

PROPEL
YOUR BUSINESS FORWARD!

Effective CV Writing

Resolving Office Conflict

Boost Your Concentration

Find Your Work-Life Balance

www.50minutes.com

GETTING THINGS DONE AND STAYING ORGANISED

- **Problem:** how can you better organise your workload?
- **Uses:** good organisation at work is the key to efficiency: it allows you to reduce the chance of unexpected events whilst saving your energy.
- **Professional context:** personal organisation, organisation within the company, internal communication, delegation.
- **FAQ:**
  - Where do I begin?
  - How can I spot the obstacles to good organisation?
  - How can I regulate stress that prevents me from working?
  - What is the role of delegation in the organisation of work?
  - Organisation and communication: do they go hand in hand?
  - How can I optimise my time?
  - How can I manage my priorities?

Do you feel overwhelmed or swamped by the number of things you need to do at work today? Do you not even know where to start, even though the stress is beginning to overwhelm you? This means that you urgently need to get organised, before things get out of control!

Organisation is actually a tool for wellbeing at work, which means that you will be less stressed and more efficient in your tasks. In a professional environment that is certain to demand more and more from you, where time is broken up and tasks are endless, being able to intelligently organise your work becomes almost a condition of survival.

Good organisation is acquired through the use of tools, but also through self-awareness with regard to your values, needs and limitations. As such, in this book you will find the key to better organisation, which is tailored to your personal functioning.

The objective is to implement 'green' organisation, meaning organisation that suits you, through an overall reflection on your personality and the tools that you will be using, as well as your working environment (your colleagues and the company's values). This way, you will not have to force things and your professional circle will see you as incredibly efficient!

FEATURES OF A WELL-ORGANISED WORKER

FRAMEWORK SET BY THE COMPANY

You are probably not responsible for the organisational framework of your company, but you do have to live with it. It therefore plays an important part in arranging your personal workload. This framework is designed in the interests of a company, as it allows it to optimise its operation and costs, but it is also intended to benefit people, by respecting each individual within that company.

Thus, organisation appears to be a strong point of communication within a company, as it establishes a protocol that allows each service and each individual to speak the same language. For this protocol to be implemented, it must be precise and comprehensible, i.e. simple, logical and easily transmitted. It must also be a source of inspiration for each individual organisation and serve as an example or guideline for them to follow.

This is explained by Pierre-Marie Gadonneix, administrative and financial director at *ITV Studios France*, who has experienced strong human resource development in his company over the last few years.

> "Our ultimate aim is to produce television programmes. Organisation is therefore paramount as it is a way of optimising the primary function of the company. Cost optimisation requires more efficient organisation to allow for maximum

> respect of the human resources function. We must make sure that the pressure required for the function does not negatively affect the working atmosphere.
>
> [...]
>
> There cannot be multiple operating systems within a company. It is important to establish common processes to which every employee adheres, right from recruitment. Otherwise, this not only creates practical problems for projects, but also tension within the team."

KNOW YOURSELF

Values

Our values make us who we are on a very fundamental level: they are embedded in us. They give meaning to our actions and lead us to act with all the strength we are capable of. It is therefore essential to know how to make best use of these fundamentals. We are naturally more efficient at tasks that are consistent with our values. Conversely, if our values do not line up with tasks, each of them requires considerable effort, often leading us to postpone them until later (procrastination), hoping that we will eventually find the motivation.

Depending on the physical or psychological situation in which we find ourselves, we draw more or less on a specific value. This means that we constantly review our scale of values, so it is important to regularly re-examine what is important to us.

Becoming aware of the values that sustain us enables us to prioritise tasks and thus to organise ourselves more naturally. Pay attention to your desires, because the tasks you want to do will be completed with greater speed and ease. But do not forget to buckle down occasionally (when your energy level is at its highest) to tackle the less rewarding tasks...

SELF-REFLECTION

- What are your values? They could include family, friends, work, contribution to society, sport, respect, social success, honesty, sharing. Write down everything that matters to you.
- Rank them in order of importance: try to determine the values that influence the majority of your actions and behaviours.
- How does your work contribute to them? What could you do differently to achieve greater personal integrity?

Limits

Knowing yourself is also about knowing your limits. These must be taken into consideration when getting organised. We all have 'helping' limits, those that allow us to respect and be compassionate with ourselves, and 'limiting' limits, which prevent us from acting or carrying out an action. They either protect us or hold us back. It is therefore important to identify them in order to turn them into a strength for our organisation. Ask yourself the following questions:

- "What are my 'helping' limits, those that protect me,

preserve my energy and allow me to be consistent with myself and evolve?"

- ○ Example: I only accept physical contact, such as a hand placed on my shoulder, from my close friends.
- "Conversely, what are my 'limiting' limits, which restrict me and prevent me from moving forward?"
  - ○ Example: I usually stay silent during group meetings; I prefer to let others talk.
- "What are the limits I impose upon others? Do I formulate them clearly?"
- "What do I do when a person crosses my limits? Do I react in a way that makes them understand?"

By answering these questions and defining these elements, you will be clear with yourself and farsighted in your actions. You will be a reliable guide for implementing coherent and organised actions.

It is also necessary to lay down these limits to others, in order to be consistent with your professional circle. For this, an essential relational competence is required: being able to say no. Jacques Salomé, a French psychologist and writer, explains that saying no to somebody else means saying yes to yourself. Knowing when to say no is one of the keys to good personal organisation and contributes to personal development. By refusing some things, you avoid letting others control your actions and can be consistent with yourself: it helps you to distinguish between your priorities and those of others. Saying no is also easier to do when you clearly recognise the needs you say yes to!

SOMETHING TO REMEMBER

Being available to others is obviously an excellent quality, but only if it does not stop you from doing what the company hired you to do. Moreover, a person who can say no to some requests with tact and firmness gives more value to their yes and will be more recognised and appreciated. This is not a sign of a disagreement or conflict, but the manifestation of a difference and an openness to the possibility of a real exchange.

TIME MANAGEMENT

Good practices and causes of inefficiency

Each individual has their own perception of time. It is therefore important to take stock of your own perception of time and how you manage it. By listing your strengths and weaknesses, you will be able to identify the good practices that you have acquired, but also the causes of inefficiency in the way you work.

That way, you can highlight some strengths, such as always being punctual at meetings you are invited to, and some weak points, such as the fact that you are always in a hurry, which gives the impression that you do not take care in your work.

- For each weakness identified, ask yourself where it comes from. In the case mentioned above, the problem may be that you forget to complete certain tasks early on:

you are relying on your memory, even though it can let you down! That said, you are now able to implement a solution to your problem, by determining a precise and measurable action: using a support that will allow you to remember events or things to do at time T, for example. The only thing left for you to do is choose the most appropriate support for your mode of operation: post-it notes, notebook, exercise book, personal organiser or any other tool of your choice that is both convenient and easily accessible.

- As for the best practices that you have observed, be aware of them and do not hesitate to draw from them to find solutions to your inefficiencies. As the saying from Zen Buddhism goes: "Look for what you are lacking in that which you already have."

Biological rhythm

It is now scientifically proven: we have internal rhythms that are worth knowing and listening to. During a day, our body temperature varies, as does our muscle strength and brain activity. Thus, all the functions of our body work with these ups and downs.

While it is recognised that efficiency is at its highest between 10:00am and 11:00am and between 3:00pm and 4:30pm, take the time to identify your most efficient hours, during which your mind is very alert, and your off-peak hours, during which your physiological needs – hunger, fatigue, and so on – decrease your performance. Observing your behaviour over one day will be the most effective method for reviewing these more and less productive periods.

To use your biorhythm as an asset to your organisation, consider these cycles when allocating the different tasks you have to perform in a day. You will now simply schedule tasks that require greater intellectual availability into the time slots during which you know you are the most alert, meaning you will be all the more efficient.

OBSTACLES

Distractions

External obstacles and distractions affect professional performance. Unsurprisingly, among them we find those factors that disturb our senses: noise, temperature, bad ergonomics in the workplace, and so on. Make sure that your environment does not disturb your concentration. Aerate your desk at least once a day and do not hesitate to close the door or listen to music through headphones to isolate yourself when you need to.

EXTRA INFORMATION

Make your workstation your own: during the week, you will spend the majority of your time there, so give it a little something to make it familiar and make you feel good, such as putting a small plant or personal object on your desk.

Professional interactions

As other people constantly ask things of us (by phone, email, requests for help, and so on), it is relatively rare that we will not be interrupted in our work. Indeed, we need to always be open to others, so it is often difficult to carry out a task from start to finish without having to respond to external demands.

For example, the temptation is to immediately view the contents of an email upon receipt, and maybe even answer it. However, it is better to take the time to correctly answer each message, rather than deal with it briefly and only provide a partial or unhelpful response such as, "I will check and get back to you." No doubt the other person will be glad to see that their request is being considered, but they still do not have their answer and they will probably have interrupted their task to read your message, just as you had done to answer them.

Start by establishing rules on the use of communication tools. For example, choose to check your inbox a maximum of four or five times a day, at more or less regular intervals: in the morning on your arrival, mid-morning, midday on returning from your break, mid-afternoon and 30 minutes before you leave in the evening.

These tips also apply to using your smartphone: possessing

one does not mean you have to be permanently contac-
table. After all, inboxes are very good at their jobs! You can
check your messages and call people back after you have
completed the task you are focusing on. Again, you will be
able to provide a better answer if your mind is not busy with
other things.

Stress

Not all obstacles come from outside; some, which are very
disabling, are hidden within us. The most widespread and
destructive of all is, undoubtedly, stress.

Stress is a dramatisation of the future. When we are
stressed, our mental state is affected: our behaviour, emotions and moods can swing from rational to irrational and
our actions lose their consistency, sometimes to the point
of completely paralysing us.

Stress at work is not inevitable and you can work around
it. The key is defining what is and is not your responsibility.
Imagine three zones around you in which you will place the
tasks you must perform:

- Your impact zone. This is the closest zone to you, where
  your actions and decisions have a direct effect.
- Your influence zone. This is a little further away from you.
  You can act in this zone but will not be able to directly
  affect the objective. However, your actions can have an
  influence.
- The zone that is out of your reach. This zone is too far
  from you and you have no control over what happens

there, whatever action you decide to take.

Each zone is likely to generate stress, including the farthest zone. However, this zone is out of your reach: you cannot do anything to change the situation. It is therefore better to stop worrying and focus on your zones of impact and influence. By acting as best you can in these zones, you will be able to channel your emotions better and prevent stress from mounting.

For example: you are flying to meet several major clients in another country, and your flight is delayed by two hours, which inevitably makes you late for the entire day. Instead of getting worked up, realise that this delay is beyond your control: you cannot do anything to make the plane arrive sooner (outside of your impact). However, what you do during this waiting time is entirely up to you (impact zone). Concentrate on this and do not put unnecessary pressure on yourself about a delay that is not your fault.

Stay calm

- Look at things as they are, without emotional interference: distinguish between the objective facts and your feelings related to these facts.
- Be in the present: this will stop you from anticipating a possible negative outcome that will stress you beforehand. Instead of thinking "If I do this, this could happen", say "Today I am acting according to this valid goal, and I am expecting these results", and keep in mind that no one can predict

everything.

Procrastination

Procrastination is a symptom that involves putting off to tomorrow what could or should be done today. This art of putting things off mainly manifests when too many things need to be done all at the same time, or when you have to do something that goes against your values. You then constantly think about what you should be doing, without finding the energy to actually do it.

Begin by remembering this principle: if you have all the necessary information, immediate action is always quicker and often more effective than doing it later.

Now, if it is absolutely necessary to postpone things until the next day, the best solution is to make this tendency to procrastinate a positive and creative tool by considering the future consequences of postponing each action, both for you and your professional circle. This will allow you to prioritise more easily. Ask yourself for which task may have the most serious consequences and focus on this task, leaving others for later.

WARNING!

Do not forget to find a spare moment later in the week or the month to complete all those little things you left out – no excuses this time!

PRIORITISING TASKS

After exploring the internal factors of developing your personal organisation, it is now important to prioritise your tasks. Some need to be done before others due to their priority level. This seems obvious, but it is not so easy to implement, as to do so you have to be able to distinguish between what is important and what is urgent, and not confuse speed with efficiency.

For this, it is easier to proceed step by step. Again, taking one step after another, you will take giant leaps forward and, most importantly, advance in the right direction.

- For each project you are involved in, start by clearly identifying the tasks that come back to you personally. Break down the demanding and complex activities into different, more feasible parts.

EXTRA INFORMATION

For each project, ask yourself the following three questions:

- What is my role?
- What falls under my responsibility?
- What specific actions need to be taken?

- List them, whether on a piece of paper or in a table on your computer, in order to be aware of the scope of actions needed for each project. For this list to be effective, each task should begin with a verb that calls for action.

- Then, sort the tasks according to their urgency and importance, giving a number to each one. This will allow you to take into account the logic of the sequence of events as well as what agrees with your values, and the expectations and needs of your colleagues and managers. For example: No. 1 – contact suppliers; No. 2 – identify customer needs; and so on.
- All that remains now is to schedule tasks over time, by roughly estimating the time required to complete each one. It is important to update your calendar, leaving yourself some room for manoeuvre in case of unexpected mishaps. The result will be something like this: Monday and Tuesday – contact suppliers; Wednesday – identify needs; and so on. Review your plan as often as necessary.

In case you have difficulty in planning certain tasks as they all seem urgent, return to the previous step and review your classification. Ask yourself if a task can wait until the following day or the following week. If necessary, and if you think it acceptable, do not hesitate to ask, as soon as possible, for additional time from your client or supervisor.

Take responsibility for yourself and try to finish the tasks scheduled for each day. The benefit will be immediate: a feeling of intense satisfaction with the work done. And if you notice that you are falling behind, return to your schedule and adjust it to suit reality.

KNOW HOW TO DELEGATE!

Now that you have a clear vision of the work that awaits you, you may realise that you will need to tap into other resources if you want everything to be done in time.

Indeed, delegating allows you to distribute the workload and favours initiative. This helps to develop true teamwork, improved productivity and a form of recognition for everyone. By delegating, you define your role, position yourself in relation to others and thus encourage others to accept responsibility. It is therefore a key element in both your own organisation and that of the company.

Pierre-Marie Gadonneix told us:

> "I am copied into all e-mails but I don't intervene unless the recipients ask me directly. I delegate, which gives me time to take a step back and work on less functional aspects."

"What can I delegate?"

Eisenhower matrix

The Eisenhower matrix allows us to answer this question. Accomplish the tasks you deem urgent and important yourself, but do not hesitate to delegate those you consider as important but less urgent, or those that are urgent but less important.

Keep in mind that delegating also takes time in planning and communication, which is why it is better to directly transmit fairly heavy or repetitive tasks that justify the time taken upstream.

"To whom should I delegate?"

To distinguish the right person for a delegated project, it is also necessary here to proceed step by step. You need to:

- Assess the task to be delegated;
- Identify the skills and responsibilities required for its completion;
- Choose a skilled and motivated person. You can also simply consider their potential, providing them with further training if necessary.

> **WARNING!**
>
> Do not delegate at random. By basing delegation on an approximate and subjective evaluation of an employee and assuming that they will be delighted with this delegation, you may lose time rather than gain it if it turns out you were wrong; then you will most likely need to re-check the work completed.

"How do I delegate well?"

Successful delegation requires suitable communication. To do this, focus on all three modes of communication:

- reporting, or upward information from contributor to the delegator;
- debriefing, or exchange on the same level for the different contributors;
- appraisal, or downward information from delegator to

the contributor.

Through these techniques, you will be able to delegate a project efficiently by following these steps:

- Define a clear and precise objective to be communicated and respected. This requires a mutual commitment on the resources and clearly defined responsibilities.
- Delegation must be in congruence with the objective and in harmony with the expectations of the employee, while respecting their interests. It must be a win-win exchange. You delegate a task to achieve a goal that has been set for you. The employee must also benefit from it: feeling that they are the right person to perform the task, showing their investment and skills, but also proving that they are able to excel. Pay attention to possible resistance as well as excessive enthusiasm, and treat them with the right amount of understanding and/or firmness.
- Check in regularly, without micromanaging. Control allows for modifying an action undertaken if necessary, congratulating, initiating additional action, or adding or removing resources, and so on.
- Stop trying to take over and do things yourself. You have your way of doing things and your employee perhaps has a slightly different way. Let it go! The important thing is that the employee has understood the goal you have set for them and all the parameters involved in achieving it.
- Pay attention to your communication, whether upstream, downstream, or during the execution of the delegated task. Have you prepared the foundation of your delegation well? The communication you establish

beforehand will be useful during and after the task.
- Remember to conclude the experience with a post-delegation discussion. Providing the employee with feedback on their work is of paramount importance for their development and adhesion with the company.

WARNING!

- Do not delegate in a hurry as you may skip a step or poorly communicate the goal.
- Do not be a perfectionist: know how to let go regarding methods that may be different from yours, but just as effective. Too much control leads to disempowerment and a loss of motivation.

TOP TIPS

- Avoid clutter, which is the enemy of organisation: sort as you go along. A tidy desk when you leave in the evening is a welcoming desk the next morning and a good start to the day.
- Arrange your workstation ergonomically. Minimise the movement you have to make by keeping to hand the files or tools you need several times a day. Organise everything in a simple and convenient way to quickly find what you are looking for. For example, a folder that is sorted into a pocket in a folder that is in a drawer requires too many movements. Excessive movements are both a waste of time and energy, and a loss of concentration if you find yourself cursing as you cannot find the document you are looking for.
- Be understandable and intelligible to yourself and your colleagues, as much in oral communication as in written: a folder name defined according to a common classification saves everyone time.
- Clarify your plans and support your intentions by setting concrete sub-objectives in order to see more clearly. Break up demanding and complex activities as much as possible into different, more feasible parts.
- Be aware of your responsibilities. Taking responsibility for a task and defining its limits will prevent you from taking on other people's work, which will cause you unnecessary stress, as it does not fall within your domain of action.
- Enter the recurring events of your work over the month or year into your calendar. This will allow you to anticipate

and prepare for these tasks;

- Enter only professional and essential things into your diary. It is needless to overload your professional calendar with a birthday reminder: this visual confusion may damage your motivation and energy.
- Estimate the time required to carry out your tasks. When starting a new task, you must know the time you will dedicate to it and stick to that limit. If you do not have an exact idea of the time needed, note the time you started a task and the time you finished it. This will allow you to use this as an estimate for the next time.
- Similarly, set yourself deadlines: this will allow you to set up an action plan for your day or week based on your priorities.
- Prepare for your meetings: agenda, list of participants, questions, key points, and so on.
- Be aware of the resources that you need to be effective. Choose the right tools and train yourself to use them: lost time and stress are often consequences of unsuitable tools or tools that you are not comfortable using. Do not hesitate to ask more experienced colleagues who can give you a few minutes of informal training on the use of a tool, rather than continuing to have difficulty every day with the same task.
- Take breaks! This may seem paradoxical, but taking a five-minute break every two hours can save you time. In fact, your brain cannot maintain maximum activity for the whole day. Give it time to recharge and start afresh.

FAQS

WHERE DO I BEGIN?

It is essential to start by working on yourself. Observing yourself and your activity is the essential way of establishing good organisation. Check the values that support you as well as the limits you do not wish to cross.

Based on these values and limits, you will be able to identify the tasks that motivate you and for which you are likely to be most effective, and the tasks that will require additional effort. You will be able to justify a "no" when faced with a request that crosses your limits.

HOW CAN I SPOT THE OBSTACLES TO GOOD ORGANISATION?

To locate these obstacles that originate both outside and inside of ourselves, we must first observe, listen to and sense the things around us.

- Is your seat adjusted to the correct height?
- Are your screen and keyboard well-positioned?
- Is your phone easily accessible? Is the handset suitable?
- Is there noise around you? If so, what resources do you have to better isolate yourself?
- Is the room temperature often a topic of discussion? If it is often cold, do you have a jacket you can leave on the back of your chair? Or, if it is often hot, have you thought of aerating the room?

Gradually, by rectifying these elements that may seem like small details, you will feel much more comfortable in your working environment. This is the first step towards efficiency.

Continue by analysing your interactions with others (colleagues, superiors, clients, suppliers, and so on): are they distracting? If so, how can you optimise them so that your concentration is affected as little as possible? Relate these thoughts to the use of your tools (computer, laptop, and so on) so you can balance the two.

With regard to internal obstacles, your tendency to procrastinate is easily spotted if you were supposed to write a report two months ago or tidy up the material used at the latest event, but have not done any of it. If this is the case, it is time to take the bull by the horns and immediately start thinking about the best way to deal with these small tasks that are repeatedly postponed.

Finally, learn to read the signals that indicate stress: troubled sleep or frequent insomnia; noticeable tiredness; backaches; anxiety about the future; and so on. By becoming aware of these signs, you will be able to react before becoming overwhelmed.

HOW CAN I REGULATE STRESS THAT PREVENTS ME FROM WORKING?

You have determined what is and is not situated in your impact zone, yet your stress continues to overwhelm you in the face of the mountain of tasks you need to complete in a period of time that is getting shorter and shorter. To help you monitor stress, begin by identifying its sources in your work:

- Is it related to the content of your work? Workload, task complexity, monotony, level of responsibility, level of autonomy, professional risks, pace of work, pressure, and so on.
- Is it related to your working environment? Atmosphere (noise, temperature, brightness, and so on), workstation layout, company size and structure, colleagues, superior hierarchy, and so on.

Once the sources of stress have been identified, you have to learn how to react calmly to them. It is preferable for this to be organised in order to stay in a comfort zone that is defined by three elements:

- Security. As a priority, select the areas where you feel safe, just to gradually regain confidence in yourself.
- Legitimacy. If you are asked to adopt a new behaviour that you cannot view as legitimate, do not change. Any changes must closely link your behaviour to your values to have any chance of success.
- Ease. When you have taken the first step, you have built a solid base for the second. Choose ease and guarantee success!

Now, take action! Focus on the next thing you need to do, not the final work that must be done or the objective that must be achieved. To do this, think in terms of ACTIONS! Instead of focusing on the mountain before you, consider the tangible facts: plan concrete and doable tasks, such as "learn about competitors" or "make a first selection from the applications received". Once the task is completed, move on to the next, and so on. Gradually, the work will progress and stress will decrease.

WHAT IS THE ROLE OF DELEGATION IN THE ORGANISATION OF WORK?

Delegating less important or less urgent tasks allows you to make time for those that are really worth your personal effort. You can also decide to delegate the tasks for which you have fewer skills than your colleagues. This will save everyone time: for you personally and for the project in general.

Being able to delegate effectively is a key element of good work organisation. To do this:

- evaluate the work and skills required in order to wisely choose which person to entrust with the task;
- define a clear and specific goal with them, then give them free rein on how to achieve it while ensuring the regular monitoring of the task;
- circulate information before, during and after the delegation, through reporting, debriefing and appraisal;
- measure achievement by passing on a report, allowing you to show your appreciation of your employee and thereby influence their motivation.

ORGANISATION AND COMMUNICATION: DO THEY GO HAND IN HAND?

Whenever you want to set up a project that requires several skills, want to delegate or are facing a conflict, you will need to communicate. It is therefore essential to be responsible for your communication and to control it so that it is not an obstacle when the time comes for organisation.

Thus, openness to others, active listening, the ability to read paraverbal and nonverbal language, the reformulation of information and the art of questioning are all part of the key tools for effective communication.

Some guidelines to keep in mind and implement

- I consider and appreciate the other person for their true value.
- I keep a certain emotional distance to maintain my neutrality.
- I only listen to needs that are relevant to the situation and put others aside. This means that I stay focused on good intentions and remain lucid.
- My intentions are clear, which inspires confidence.
- I circulate information in both directions: in this way, I feed the movement required for communication.

'Anti-communication'

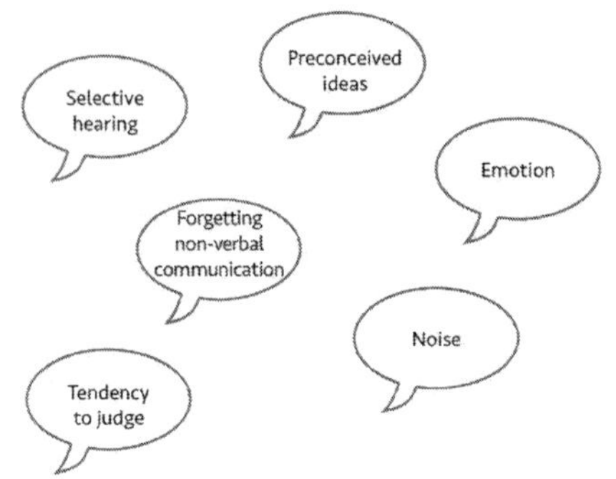

HOW CAN I OPTIMISE MY TIME?

Time is precious in days that are often very busy. Analyse your relationship with time in order to draw the right conclusions on points that need to be improved.

Be aware of your strengths as well as your sources of inefficiency in order to work on them. To identify them, answer the following questions in order:

- Is it difficult for you to manage the time allotted for performing a particular task?
- If so, what are the difficulties you encounter most often?

- What makes you experience this difficulty?
- What consequences does this have on your organisation?

Listing your difficulties allows you to propose a solution for each of them and highlight the benefits this will bring you.

Another way to optimise working time is to plan your day according to your biological rhythm. Make optimal use of your hours of full concentration by filling them with the tasks that require more of your intellect. If your activity requires you to stay very concentrated until 1:00pm, there is nothing stopping you from anticipating your loss of energy and having a snack at around 10:00am.

HOW CAN I MANAGE MY PRIORITIES?

Priorities are defined by two poles: yourself and your environment. Knowing how to manage them involves:

- Distinguishing between urgent and important tasks. Urgent tasks have to be completed, but never at the expense of important tasks. To do this, always schedule at least one major task to perform each day.
- Striking the right balance between what you are asked to do and what you feel is right. Consider the issue as a whole, trying to estimate if what is asked of you is important in view of your objectives or those of your team. Then know how to expose your perception of things to your colleagues and superiors – as the importance of a task can sometimes be subjective – and be able to say no or to request additional time when it risks affecting your work.

To summarise, act in descending order: first deal with the tasks which will have serious consequences for your work and that of your colleagues if they are not completed, then the tasks that are important or urgent, then those whose consequences are more limited, and so on.

OVER TO YOU

Here are some very simple exercises that will help you to become aware of your current situation, propose your own solutions in relation to different areas for improvement and thus develop effective and efficient organisation.

TIME MANAGEMENT

Objective: Identify what reduces your effectiveness in time management.

List your weaknesses in a table. For each one, note the reason and your proposed solution. In order to set a measurable goal, plan a deadline for implementing the solution.

Time management

Weaknesses	Reasons	Solutions	Deadline for resolution

Stay organized © 50MINUTES.com

PRIORITISING

Objective: Analyse the tasks performed and those that have not been done over a day, and their level of priority.

List in one table the tasks performed in a day hour by hour, then, in a second table, the tasks that you did not manage to complete.

Completed tasks

Time	Completed tasks	Priority
7:00		
8:00		
...		
...		
...		
19:00		

Stay organized © 50MINUTES.com

Uncompleted tasks

Time	Uncompleted tasks	Priority
7:00		
8:00		
...		
...		
...		
19:00		

Stay organized © 50MINUTES.com

On this basis, answer the following two questions and, depending on the answers, possibly re-evaluate the priority of certain tasks:

- What consequences did the uncompleted tasks have on your working day?
- How could you have acted differently?

OBSTACLES

Objective: Re-energise by deciding to eliminate obstacles.

In a table, list at least three things that interfere with your work organisation every day and waste your energy. Then take the time to think about what you could do to reduce the negative effects of these distractions.

Obstacles

Obstacle			
Cost			
Proposed action			
Expected benefits			
Predicted date			
Actual date			

Stay organized © 50MINUTES.com

STRESS

Objectives: Refocus your energy on your impact zone by classifying the different stress factors.

List the stressors encountered during a day's work: those that you perceive as positive (new projects, training an intern in addition to your usual work, etc.) and those that you perceive as negative (pressure, conflict, etc.).

Position these factors in one of the following three circles:

Zones

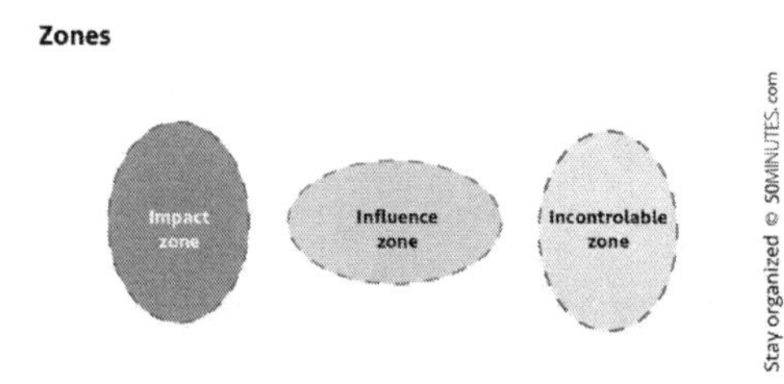

Finally, consider the negative stress factors that are within your area of influence and of impact: starting now, what can you do to reduce your stress and increase your energy?

We want to hear from you!
Leave a comment on your online library
and share your favourite books on social media!

FURTHER READING

BIBLIOGRAPHY

- Salomé, J. (2008) *À qui ferais-je de la peine si j'étais moi-même ?* Montreal: Les Éditions de l'Homme.

50MINUTES.com

History
Business
Coaching
Book Review
Health & Wellbeing

IMPROVE YOUR
GENERAL KNOWLEDGE
IN A BLINK OF AN EYE !

www.50minutes.com

Although the editor makes every effort to verify the accuracy of the information published, 50Minutes.com accepts no responsibility for the content of this book.

© **50MINUTES.com, 2016. All rights reserved.**

www.50minutes.com

Ebook EAN: 9782806269751

Paperback EAN: 9782806270733

Legal Deposit: D/2015/12603/450

Cover: © Primento

Digital conception by Primento, the digital partner of publishers.

Made in the USA
Monee, IL
08 July 2026